W9-BEA-137

PENGUINS

LIVING WILD

Published by Creative Education
P.O. Box 227, Mankato, Minnesota 56002
Creative Education is an imprint of The Creative Company

Design and production by Mary Herrmann
Art direction by Rita Marshall
Printed in the United States of America

Photographs by Dreamstime (Aneurysm, Bernardbreton, Cascoly, Csakisti, Enjoylife25, Musat, Vladsilver), Getty Images (Ira Block, Bill Curtsinger/National Geographic, Tui De Roy, Daisy Gilardini, Johnny Johnson, Ross Land, Ty Milford, Flip Nicklin, Ingrid Visser/Foto Natura, Ian Waldie, Konrad Wothe, Norbert Wu), iStockphoto (Lynsey Allan, Heather Faye Bath, Steve Estvanik, Eric Gevaert, Jeff Goldman, David T Gomez, Alexander Hafemann, Ian Johnson, Grigory Kubatyan, Erlend Kvalsvik, Nataliya Lamonova, Dawn Nichols, Maxim Pometun, James Richey, Wolfgang Schoenfeld, Andr? Sch?fer, Mark Skinner, Vance Smith, Wayne Tam, JOSE TEJO, Jan Will)

Library of Congress Cataloging-in-Publication Data
Hanel, Rachael.
Penguins / by Rachael Hanel.
p. cm. — (Living wild)
Includes index.
ISBN 978-1-58341-658-7
1. Penguins—Juvenile literature. I. Title. II. Series.

QL696.S473H36 2008
598.47—dc22   2007008503

9 8 7 6 5 4 3

C CREATIVE EDUCATION

PENGUINS

Rachael Hanel

A penguin walking on land makes
for an amusing sight. It waddles

and sways back and forth, as if it
could fall over at any moment.

A penguin walking on land makes for an amusing sight. It waddles and sways back and forth, as if it could fall over at any moment. Its feet shuffle forward timidly like an unsteady person. When it gets tired of walking, it may lie down and scoot across the Antarctic ice on its belly, looking like a toboggan. But in the ocean, the penguin is truly at home. The feet that were clumsy on land function in the water as a **rudder** that guides the penguin's direction, making its movements in the water graceful and smooth. The wings that were useless in the air become strong propellers in the ocean, helping the penguin dive for food in the cold, dark depths of the sea. This is where the penguin is most comfortable, and it stays in and close to water for many months of the year.

WHERE IN THE WORLD THEY LIVE

■ **Emperor Penguin**
Antarctica

□ **Gentoo Penguin**
Antarctica and subantarctic islands

■ **King Penguin**
subantarctic islands

■ **Chinstrap Penguin**
Antarctica

■ **Macaroni Penguin**
subantarctic islands

■ **Royal Penguin**
subantarctic islands

■ **Rockhopper Penguin**
islands off southern tip of South America and throughout subantarctic

Humboldt Penguin
coast of Peru in South America

Penguins are found only in the Southern Hemisphere, below the equator. These colored dots represent their primary breeding grounds, or where they live for most of the year.

■ **Erect-crested Penguin (not pictured)**
four small islands southeast of New Zealand

□ **African Penguin**
southern tip of Africa

■ **Magellanic Penguin**
coasts of Chile and Argentina in South America

□ **Galápagos Penguin**
Galápagos Islands, just below equator

■ **Adélie Penguin**
Antarctica

■ **Yellow-eyed Penguin**
eastern New Zealand

■ **Fairy Penguin**
southern Australia and eastern New Zealand

□ **Snares Penguin**
Snares Island, south of New Zealand

□ **Fiordland Penguin**
southwestern New Zealand

MADE FOR THE WATER

Emperor penguins are known for their large size.

E ven though it does not fly, the penguin is classified as a bird, *Sphenisciformes spheniscidae*. Like most birds, penguins have feathers, horny beaks with no teeth, and eggs with large yolks and hard shells. Their closest living relatives are flying birds that also prey on fish, such as albatrosses and petrels.

Penguins are most often associated with the icy expanses of Antarctica. However, penguins are found throughout the Southern Hemisphere. They live in New Zealand, Australia, and at the southern tips of South America and Africa. They also make their homes on the many islands found in the Southern Hemisphere. One species, the Galápagos penguin, lives in the tropical waters of the equator alongside turtles, sea lions, and sharks.

The big, black-and-white emperor penguin is probably the best-known species. But there are 16 other species of penguin, and they all look different. The biggest penguin is the emperor, which weighs 66 to 84 pounds (30–38 kg). The tiniest species, appropriately called the little blue or fairy, weighs only around two and a half pounds (1.1 kg).

Penguins are versatile birds. They have adapted to a wider range of climates on Earth than any other species.

The banded African penguins live on the tip of South Africa.

In the 1990s, amendments to the global Antarctic Treaty, first signed in 1959, protected all penguins in and surrounding Antarctica, including the tip of South America.

The 17 penguin species are divided into six groups. The two largest penguins, the emperor and the king, make up one group. The crested penguins—identified by a ridge of feathers on their heads—include the royal, macaroni, rockhopper, erect-crested, Fiordland, and Snares. The banded penguins are marked by a stripe across their chests and include the Humboldt, African, Magellanic, and Galápagos. The Adélie, the chinstrap, and the gentoo are in the brush-tailed group because their tails are longer and look like little brushes. Two groups have just one species apiece—the yellow-eyed penguin and the little blue penguin.

Regardless of species, all penguins have uniquely designed bodies that help them navigate ocean waters and stay cool or warm, depending upon their habitat. Like a strong ship, a penguin is made to swim effortlessly through the sea. Its short legs and feet are positioned far back on the body. This is why penguins waddle awkwardly on land. But in the water, the legs, feet, and tail combine to make a powerful rudder that steers a penguin precisely in any direction.

A penguin's flippers, or wings, are short and broad, like canoe oars. The oar-like wings help a penguin slice

Currently, it is estimated that there are 2.23 million pairs of king penguins living in the subantarctic.

Humboldt penguins are named for the German scientist, Alexander von Humboldt, who first described them.

through the water and propel it forward. Unlike other birds, a penguin's bones are heavy. Birds that fly have hollow skeletons that allow them to flit lightly through the air. A penguin's dense skeleton allows it to stay submerged under water.

Although each species of penguin looks a little different from another, all of them have a dark-colored back and light-colored front. Scientists believe this provides **camouflage** in the water. If a predator from the air looks down into the water, the black of a penguin's back blends in with the murky depths of the ocean. If a predator deep in the ocean looks up at a penguin from below, the white of the front blends with the sun's light shining into the water.

The one body part that helps penguins when they are on land is their feet. Penguins have webbed feet, which provides resistance in the water while swimming. But the feet also have three claw-like toes that are used for gripping ice and rocks on land. Sometimes penguins will also use their beaks to get a good hold when climbing up rocks.

Penguins, whether they live in a warm climate or a cold one, can regulate their body temperature. Generally,

penguins that live in and near Antarctica are larger
than penguins that live farther north. Their large body
mass helps them retain heat. Birds that live in the bitter
cold—where temperatures can range from -40 to -94 °F
(-40 to -70 °C) in the coldest month—are fully covered
with feathers. The feathers on cold-weather penguins are
packed closely together, leaving little room for the warm
air generated by their bodies to escape. They overlap each
other like roof shingles, which prevents strong winds
from ruffling the feathers. In addition, each feather has
a separate shaft covered with **down** that creates another

layer to trap heat. Penguins that live in cold climates store a layer of fat, called blubber, close to their skin. Blubber helps retain heat and can also be converted into energy if a penguin is not near a food source. Some penguins have a layer of blubber up to an inch (2.5 cm) thick.

Penguins that live in warm temperatures know how to stay cool. When penguins get too warm, their bodies send more blood to their flippers. The feathers on their flippers are short, which means that more of their skin is exposed to the air. The air moving over the warm skin helps to cool it. To cool down even further, a penguin will flap

To balance themselves as they unsteadily walk, penguins extend their flippers to the sides.

African penguins live on warm beaches and can move easily, as opposed to penguins in colder climates.

its wings, much like humans will use a hand-held fan, to create a cool breeze. Their bodies will also send blood to their faces. Penguins in warmer climates usually do not have feathers around the eyes or beak. The skin on the face flushes and cools, just like the skin on the flippers.

A penguin's two colors also help control its body temperature. If a penguin is cold, it can lie with its dark back to the sun and soak in the rays. Or if the penguin is already warm, turning its light-colored belly to the sun helps it stay cool.

No matter where they live, penguins **preen** themselves for hours a day to maintain the waterproofing effect of their feathers. Using its bill, a penguin takes oil from a gland just above the tail. It applies oil to its flippers, then uses its flippers to spread oil on the feathers. This oil keeps the feathers waterproof in the long days spent in the ocean. The longer the feathers are exposed to water and wind, the more quickly they wear out. They become less waterproofed and less able to protect a penguin's skin. So once or twice a year, the older feathers fall out and are replaced by new ones in a process called molting.

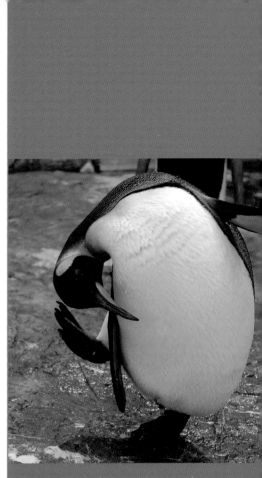

Penguins are accustomed to performing acrobatic feats in order to scratch and preen themselves.

Gentoo penguins lay two eggs in their circular nests of smooth stones, which they jealously guard.

A SOCIAL LIFE

A male penguin calls out that he has found a nesting spot.

Penguins are social creatures that prefer to spend time in groups rather than alone. Only one penguin species, the yellow-eyed penguin, spends much of its time by itself. The most important social time for penguins is the mating and breeding season, when penguins come together in large groups called **rookeries**. These rookeries can consist of hundreds, thousands, or even a million breeding pairs of penguins.

When penguins are ready to mate in the summer (which, in the Southern Hemisphere, starts around November), they leave their comfortable ocean habitat and head for land. The male penguin looks for a place to nest. Penguins that live in warmer climates will find a hole or rock crevice and fill it with bits of grass, feathers, and twigs to protect eggs from the sun. In wide-open spaces, such as in the Antarctic, penguins build a nest on the highest possible spot to protect the eggs from snow. Sometimes these nests consist of nothing more than pebbles.

Once males have found a prime nesting location, they open their beaks wide and let out a loud, shrill call. To humans, these shrieking noises sound the same. However,

Because penguins need to see both in murky water and bright sunlight, their eyes have delicate muscles that change the shape of their eye lens.

Emperor penguins protect themselves and their eggs by huddling.

Some penguins have hearty appetites. The emperor penguin can eat up to 30 pounds (14 kg) of squid or fish in one feeding.

to penguins, each call is unique; it helps the female identify her mate from the previous season. Once they pair up, a courtship between a male and female can last a few weeks.

The female of each species lays an egg or two, but what happens after that moment varies among species. Among emperor penguins, the male is responsible for **incubating** the egg. He gently places the egg on his feet, then folds a pouch of skin over it to keep the egg warm. The egg will stay there until the chick is ready to be hatched. In a delicate balancing act, the father moves cautiously and keeps the egg on his feet for several weeks. When the weather becomes harsh, all the males huddle together to keep themselves and the eggs warm.

While the father incubates the egg, the female emperor trudges back to the sea, sometimes walking up to 70 miles (113 km) or more before reaching open water at the edge of the ice shelf. There, she eats heartily, and when she's had her fill, she returns to the group several weeks later. By this time, the chick has hatched. Then it is the starving father's turn to seek food in the ocean, while the mother takes care of the new chick.

King and emperor penguins are the only species that lay and incubate just one egg at a time.

The average penguin egg hatches after 35 to 40 days, but for larger species such as the emperor, the incubation period is a long 9 weeks. When an emperor chick emerges from an egg, it looks like a round, peeping ball of fluff. All chicks are covered with downy fur that is silver, dark brown, or black. Parents take turns feeding the chick **regurgitated** food. A parent watches over the baby continuously for two to eight weeks. This is a dangerous time in the chick's life. When they are small, chicks have less protection against bitter cold, strong rain, or harsh winds. If they stray too far from their parents, they are vulnerable to attacks by hungry predators. Large birds such as skuas and giant petrels are constantly on the prowl.

After a few weeks, the chicks are old enough to be left on their own, and both parents leave to find food. In more solitary species, chicks are often left by themselves. In larger rookeries, all the chicks join together to form a **crèche**. When the parent returns, it identifies its chick by its peep.

A chick is dependent upon its parents while it still has its downy coat. The adult, waterproof feathers start to come in after a few weeks for smaller penguin species.

Emperor chicks often must wait a year before the adult feathers appear. Only when a penguin gets its feathers can it go into the water for the first time. At that time, the chicks become independent from their parents and find food for themselves.

Penguins love to eat, and they spend a majority of their time in the water swimming and searching for food. Penguins eat three types of seafood: fish, squid, and **crustaceans** such as **krill**. Stiff bristles inside a penguin's mouth help the bird grasp the slippery seafood and guide it into the stomach.

Although some penguins breed in large groups, they break into smaller groups when they reach their watery hunting grounds. Once in the water, penguins generally chase food alone. They rely on their eyesight to find food. Their eyesight is good only when there is light, so they must hunt during the day.

It is not always easy for a penguin to catch its food. The prey is usually found in large groups called schools. Once a penguin finds a school, it can feast, but it can take many days to locate such a meal. Penguins are expert divers and can plunge deep into the ocean for their food. Some can

Krill is a major food source for many ocean animals, including whales and seals.

The eggs of penguins look like other birds' eggs, except that inside, the yolk is red because krill eaten by penguins leave behind a red color.

King penguins can dive more than 350 feet (100 m) into the ocean.

Penguins spend 75 to 80 percent of their time in the ocean and may not come onto land for months at a time.

dive hundreds of feet and stay there for several minutes. They have the ability to reduce their body temperatures in the water, which lessens the need for oxygen.

Because a penguin spends most of its time in the water, that is where it faces the greatest risk from predators. Penguins can swim quickly, up to nine miles (14.5 km) per hour, but that is no match for some predators, including sea lions, seals, and sharks. However, penguins are smaller than most of their predators, so they can easily zig-zag through the water. They can also leap out of the water by using their strong flippers and legs and dive back down into a different spot.

Penguins are relatively safe on land, except for the vulnerable baby chicks. Birds such as vultures, gulls, raptors, and giant petrels have been known to nab chicks. In more temperate regions, wild animals such as dogs, **feral** cats, weasels, and foxes like to take eggs or chicks. The average life expectancy of a penguin is 15 to 20 years, though individuals in captivity can live longer.

Cold-water-loving Adélie penguins are easily recognizable by the white ring around their eyes.

Skuas are dangerous predators mainly to penguin chicks, as they eat the young of other seabirds.

CAPTURING THE IMAGINATION

When elephant seals are asleep on land, penguins have nothing to fear in walking past them.

For centuries, only the native people of New Zealand, Australia, South America, and southern Africa knew about penguins. They regularly relied on the bird's meat, skin, and feathers for food and clothing, but they were unaware of different penguins outside their own regions.

Not until the 16th century did people outside of these places happen upon penguins. European explorers sailing around the globe encountered penguins in vast numbers and were fascinated by the strange-looking creatures. In 1578, British explorer Sir Francis Drake wrote about killing 3,000 of the birds in one day at the southern tip of South America. The penguins served as a vital source of fresh meat and nourishing eggs for sailors, who often went months at sea without fresh food. Since penguins had little fear of humans, not recognizing them as predators, it was easy for sailors to get close enough to kill them. Their lack of fear left the birds vulnerable to later hunters and egg collectors as well.

Killing penguins for food did not negatively affect their populations at first. However, once people

discovered they could harvest oil from penguin blubber, the slaughter of penguins became common in the late 19th and early 20th centuries. Penguin oil was used as a base for paints, for **tanning** leather, and as lamp fuel.

Royal penguins living on Macquarie Island, off New Zealand, were a major source of oil in the 19th century. At times, up to 2,700 birds were killed each day. By 1920, public protests convinced government officials to declare the island a penguin **sanctuary**. In other areas, so many

penguins were killed that extinction became a realistic possibility. But again, public protest was enough to stop the oil harvesting, as well as the fact that man-made chemicals were being developed to replace natural oils. This development seemed to have come just in time to save penguins from complete extinction, and they have repopulated in the decades since.

Besides oil and meat, penguins were killed for their skins, which were turned into clothing, hats, and purses. Penguin

Too small to have been hunted extensively for their skin or meat, fairy penguins' main threat is the fur seal.

In 1981, a Japanese company wanted to harvest 400,000 penguins yearly for food, oil, and clothing. Public protest stopped the plan.

feathers were sometimes used to fill mattresses. As recently as the 1950s, people could buy live Galápagos penguins for their meat at ports in Ecuador for as little as $25.

Penguin populations also suffered because of the egg harvesting that has been done both **commercially** and as a hobby. Until recently, one week in November was dedicated to gathering penguin eggs in the Falkland Islands off the coast of South America, and children even got a day off of school to take part in the tradition. However, this nearly wiped out some colonies. Isolated cases of egg collecting still occur today. Game wardens have also been known to take bribes to allow the harvesting of penguins and their eggs. Today, a few penguin species are considered rare, threatened, or at risk, though none is on an endangered species list.

The yellow-eyed penguin is classified as the rarest species. An estimated 5,000 pairs live in New Zealand, and they are constantly threatened by disease, predators, and habitat destruction. For example, the yellow-eyed penguin likes to nest in cool forests, but more and more trees are being cleared for housing and retail developments. This forces the yellow-eyed penguin onto less desirable scrubby land, which it shares with predators that prey on penguins and their eggs. Another penguin that lives off the coast of New Zealand, the Fiordland crested penguin, is also in danger and is down to an estimated 3,000 pairs.

Different conservation organizations consider different penguin species to be rare, threatened, or vulnerable. The population of the Humboldt penguin, found along the South American coasts of Peru and Chile, was estimated to be 50,000 pairs in the 1960s. Now its numbers are down to between 5,000 and 6,000 breeding pairs, with another 900 living in captivity. The Galápagos penguin is also considered threatened by some organizations.

Until the late 19th and early 20th centuries, people around the world did not know much about penguins. Then, explorers made deliberate trips to Antarctica to study the environment and its wildlife. One of the first books to include pictures and descriptions of penguins was global traveler and photographer Herbert Ponting's *The Great White South*, which was published in 1921. His film, *Ninety Degrees South: With Scott to the Antarctic*, was released in 1933 and delighted audiences with its depiction of the

Adélie chicks are the fastest growing of all penguins, soon almost eclipsing their parents in size.

Rockhoppers use their flippers to help them maneuver over rocks.

The "rockhopper" penguin gets its name from its ability to hop up cliffs that are 90 feet (27 m) high in order to reach its nest.

funny-looking creatures. Nineteenth-century poets such as American Isaac McLellan were also captivated by penguins and their exotic surroundings. When the first penguins were transported to Northern Hemisphere zoos in the 20th century, even more people got to know the unusual bird.

Although penguins exist throughout the Southern Hemisphere, people around the world quickly associated them with the Antarctic, thanks to films and books such as Ponting's. In illustrations, penguins are often pictured with polar bears, even though, in reality, they live on opposite ends of the Earth.

Penguins' quirky mannerisms have long made them a favorite subject for cartoonists to draw. The first animated penguin was cartoonist Walter Lantz's Chilly Willy in 1953. Chilly Willy wears a scarf and hat and constantly seeks ways to stay warm. Tennessee Tuxedo was also a popular cartoon penguin in the 1950s and '60s.

More recently, penguins have become a pop culture phenomenon. *March of the Penguins*, a documentary film about the emperor penguins' long trips to and from their breeding grounds, won an Academy Award for the best documentary feature of 2005. Penguins also played a

major role in the animated movie *Madagascar* in 2005, plotting an escape with other animals from New York City's Central Park Zoo. Late in 2006, the animated movie *Happy Feet* focused solely on penguins, to the delight of kids around the world.

With the success of such films, penguins appear more frequently as advertising **icons**. For decades, they have been used as popular mascots for refrigeration and freezer businesses, but now the bird's reach is expanding. They have shown up in ads for Coca-Cola, Dawn dishwashing detergent, Hallmark Cards, and even to advertise the benefits of receiving influenza shots.

African penguins, though not often portrayed in movies, are some of the most approachable penguins.

Whether on snowy land (pictured) or in the water (opposite), penguins are affected by the changing temperatures on Earth.

SAVING THE PENGUIN

Since the early 1900s, scientists have been gaining more insight into the lives and unique habits of penguins. It is thought that penguins evolved from a species of flying birds that existed between 65 and 140 million years ago and adapted sleek swimming bodies for life in the ocean. Researchers have discovered penguin fossils throughout the Southern Hemisphere estimated to be between 50 and 60 million years old. No fossils have ever been found in the Northern Hemisphere.

Scientists closely monitor penguin populations, study the effects of tourism on the birds' health, and try to discover how they adapt to their ocean environment. Scientists also want to keep a close eye on penguins because penguins are one species that is an indicator of the entire planet's health. Penguins range over a large geographic area, so they are susceptible to changes both in warm ocean waters and at the frigid Antarctic ice cap.

Studying penguins is not an easy task, though. Scientists have to go to where penguins live, whether that is in the warm areas near the equator or the bitter cold of

Some penguins are incredible travelers. Adélie penguins will travel up to 3,000 miles (4,800 km) across Antarctica to return to their spring nesting grounds.

The largest penguin fossil found—discovered in New Zealand in the late 19th century—belonged to a bird estimated to weigh 178 pounds (81 kg).

the Antarctic. However, most penguins are not afraid of humans, so they are willing to let researchers get close. Once the scientists can reach a penguin, they might place a band on its wing to track its movements by satellite. This helps scientists discover exactly where a penguin travels, and the tracking technology also monitors the temperature and climate of the area.

Declining penguin populations are always of concern to researchers, and studies continue to discover the causes and to try to reverse the trend. In the late 1990s, in the Falkland Islands off the coast of Argentina, scientists wondered why populations were declining in the gentoo, rockhopper, and Magellanic species. It became clear that the increase in commercial harvesting of fish and squid in the area reduced the amount of food available for the penguins. Scientists suggested that the Falkland Islands government place restrictions on commercial fishing. But because the fishing industry drove the Falklands' economy, the government was reluctant to restrict it. Instead, they issued squid-fishing licenses to additional countries, resulting in even more ships competing to harvest food from the ocean.

THE ALBATROSS AND THE PENGUIN

Far off in southern seas by myriads throng

Those feather'd tyrants of the surging tide,

Following the fish-shoals in their devious way,

Following the smaller wild fowl o'er the deep.

   Far off Magellan's stormy strait they swarm,

Far off the rocky rampart of Cape Horn

They hovering seek their prey, and build their nests

Along the rugged precipice of isles.

Then it is well in contemplative mood

To take a stand upon some jutting cliff

And view the rugged eyrie where they build,

Amid the granite cavities of rocks.

There they may rest, secure from harm of man,

With the broad seas around to yield them food.

   Beneath them beats the all-surrounding main,

Beyond spreads out old ocean's free domain;

Above, the skies cerulean spread a dome.

To pace the shore when the salt tides are out,

To view the color'd shells that pave the beach,

Or glean the dulse and sea-kelp of the rocks;

To sit on rocks when flows the rising tide,

Attentive to all sounds that fill the air;

To view the snowy flocks as high they rise,—

All this exalts the mind to happiest mood.

   The giant albatross of southern seas,

The cruel king of all aquatic tribes,

Hovers aloft or plunges in the deep,

Eager to tear with beak and crooked claw,

The shining fish that skim the surface wave,

Or seize the lesser sea-fowl on the wing.

   Afar from human haunt, remote from land,

They float, they drift in worlds of upper air,

Seeming to slumber without flap of wing,

And dropping seldom to the lonely shore,

Save when they come to breed and build their nests.

They roam, they rob, they never feel fatigue,—

By night, by day, forever on the wing,

Forever prowling, ever at their feasts.

   One only friend have they of all the tribe—

The clumsy penguin; they together seek

Some desolate bleak island of the sea,

And there construct their nest and rear their young.

The pelican, the cormorant and gull,

And solan goose, avoid the dangerous spot,

Where, like a vast encampment in set lines,

Like tented field, these armies of great birds,

The albatross and penguin, have their home.

Yet now those lonely haunts that once they sought,

Unknown to humankind for countless years,

Are quite forsaken, and more desert shores

They seek, secure from human harm.

Isaac McLellan Jr. (1806–99)

Emperor penguins have been observed swimming at depths of 1,755 feet (535 m) and have stayed submerged for up to 18 minutes.

Other current research investigates whether the tourism industry has a negative effect upon penguin populations. Every year, thousands of tourists flock to sanctuaries to see penguins in person. On the Otago peninsula in New Zealand, researchers discovered that the yellow-eyed penguin chicks in the sanctuary tended to weigh less than chicks in the wild. The yellow-eyed penguin is more solitary, and researchers theorize that the penguin will not come ashore to feed its chicks if it sees humans nearby. The lighter-weight chicks may have a lower chance of survival.

Recent research has also shed light on the mystery of how a penguin can dive to great depths and stay underwater. The pressure under water is 40 times greater than air pressure on land. This means that while the penguin is underwater, the pressure builds up on its internal organs. In the lungs, air is compressed, which, logically, should make it harder for oxygen to travel throughout the body and reach the bird's wings, flippers, and brain. But scientists have discovered that while diving, penguins shut off their blood supply to all organs but the heart and brain. This allows the penguin to hold its breath longer.

Even though penguins are protected by law, they still face many threats today. The birds are vulnerable to even small changes in climate. For example, thawing on the Antarctic ice shelf could endanger the emperor penguin. Solid layers of ice once found in breeding areas are now thinning, putting eggs and chicks at risk of falling into the water. But not all change is negative. In places where it is getting warmer, such as in the Antarctic peninsula, the melting ice creates more areas of open water, which means more fish are available for penguins.

But in other areas, climate changes due to weather phenomena such as **El Niño** in the Pacific Ocean can affect ocean currents, which in turn affect fish populations and the predators that prey upon those fish. For example, changing weather patterns and their effects mean that the Galápagos penguin has fewer places in which to find food. When these penguins do not get enough food, they may skip a breeding season, not molt, or fail to produce eggs.

Humans continue to pose threats to penguins today. In the water, humans do not **encroach** upon a penguin's space, but on land, both humans and birds compete for territory. As human populations increase, so does the

Without tagging penguins, scientists would not be able to obtain as much information about penguins.

Penguins often take a running start before diving into the water.

King penguins can swim up to five miles (8 km) per hour. Gentoo penguins can swim up to 15 miles (24 km) per hour.

demand for business and home development, especially along the scenic shorelines of New Zealand, Australia, Africa, and South America, where penguins also reside.

Even in the Antarctic, new science stations are putting humans in contact with penguins more than ever before. Scientists, tourists, and government officials frequently venture to nearby penguin colonies. Antarctic adventures are more common and accessible to average tourists now, and thousands travel to the South Pole each year.

Ocean pollution, especially in the form of oil spills, also threatens **aquatic** wildlife such as penguins. More **supertankers** crisscross the ocean today than ever before, always posing a risk that oil from a ship may leak into the ocean. The thick, greasy liquid clings to penguin feathers and renders the birds helpless. Penguins are more at risk from oil spills because of all the time they spend in the water. In 2000, the tanker *Treasure* sank near Cape Town, South Africa, and oiled about 20,000 unfortunate African penguins.

But the recent popularity of penguins bodes well for their survival. People around the world who perhaps did not know much about these creatures before have

Penguins can rest from a long swim without going back to shore by landing on icebergs.

been exposed to more information through movies, television, and the Internet. More than ever, conservation organizations, governments, and individuals are taking steps to protect these beautiful yet vulnerable birds. The more that people become aware of penguins and the threats against them, the more that can be done to ensure they will be on Earth for many years to come.

ANIMAL TALE: A STRANGE-LOOKING BIRD

Penguins have been known to the native people of South Africa, South America, Australia, and New Zealand for thousands of years. However, unlike most other animals around the world, few, if any, myths or legends have been created about penguins. A couple of reasons may explain this phenomenon. For one, many penguins live in the isolated regions of the Antarctic and were cut off from human life until well into the 20th century. Also, native people who lived near penguin habitats may not have had the type of contact with these birds that they had with other animals. Penguins spend most of their time in the water and come ashore only to breed. Since these Southern Hemisphere regions are isolated—particularly the islands of Australia and New Zealand—stories about penguins did not have a chance to spread to other continents.

Not until European explorers sailed throughout the Southern Hemisphere did word about the penguin spread. But at first, sailors did not know what these strange-looking creatures were; they had never seen any birds like them. The earliest records about penguins come from the 15th and 16th centuries. In their travels, sailors encountered penguins off the coasts of Africa, South America, Australia, and New Zealand. Portuguese explorer Vasco da Gama's expedition, which passed by South Africa in 1497, described penguins as "birds as big as ducks, but they cannot fly, because they have no feathers on their wings." The anonymous writer from the expedition also noted that the penguins made an unusual sound, like the braying of a mule.

While traveling with Ferdinand Magellan, an explorer who was sent on a trip around the world in 1519 by the king of Spain, Italian navigator Antonio Pigafetta kept careful notes of everything he saw and experienced. When the crew rounded the southern tip of South America, Pigafetta saw a strange bird:

> "Then following the same course toward the Antarctic Pole, coasting along the land, we discovered two islands full of geese and goslings and sea wolves. The great number of these goslings there were cannot be estimated, for we loaded all the ships with them in an hour. And these goslings are black and have feathers over their whole body of the same size and fashion, and they do not fly, and they live on fish."

The birds Pigafetta referred to as "geese and goslings" were most certainly penguins. It might seem strange that Pigafetta would mistake such a strange-looking bird as a penguin for a goose. However, some scholars have theorized that Pigafetta and his fellow travelers referred to all birds as "geese," using it as a generic term.

The word "penguin" did not come into use until the 16th century, and its meaning is still debated. Some think that when Welsh sailors saw the bird in South America, they gave it the name *pengwyn*, which means "white head." It could also come from the Spanish word *penguigo*, a name given to the now-extinct great auk of the Northern Hemisphere, a bird whose coloring was similar to the penguin's.

GLOSSARY

aquatic – of or in water

camouflage – the ability to hide, due to coloring or markings that blend in with a given environment

commercially – used for business and to gain a profit rather than for personal reasons

crèche – a protected area in which baby penguins huddle to stay safe from weather and predators

crustaceans – water creatures such as shrimp, lobster, and crabs, which have a hard outer shell

down – a layer of soft fur next to a penguin's skin that traps in heat to keep the bird warm

El Niño – a Pacific Ocean weather pattern in which winds weaken and the water becomes warmer

encroach – to intrude gradually into the space of another; going beyond prescribed boundaries

feral – an untamed animal that lives in the wild or one that leaves domestication and returns to the wild

icons – images that are generally associated with one subject

incubating – the process of keeping an egg warm and protected until it is time for a chick to emerge

krill – tiny, shrimp-like creatures that live in large groups and form the base of the Antarctic food chain

preen – a bird's act of cleaning and maintaining feathers by using its beak

regurgitated – the partially digested food brought back up from an animal's stomach

rookeries – breeding or nesting places for penguins, where they gather in large groups

rudder – a steering mechanism that helps guide a ship through the water

sanctuary – a place of refuge and protection

supertankers – large ships that carry cargo such as oil throughout the world

tanning – a process by which animal skins are made into leather

SELECTED BIBLIOGRAPHY

Chester, Jonathan. *The World of the Penguin*. San Francisco: Sierra Club Books, 1996.

Fontanel, Beatrice. *The Penguin: A Funny Bird*. Watertown, Mass.: Charlesbridge, 2004.

Lynch, Wayne. *Penguins!* Willowdale, Ontario, Canada: Firefly Books, 1999.

Rivolier, Jean. *Emperor Penguins*. London: Elek Books, 1956.

Simpson, George Gaylord. *Penguins: Past and Present, Here and There*. New Haven, Conn.: Yale University Press, 1976.

Webb, Sophie. *My Season with Penguins: An Antarctic Journal*. Boston: Houghton Mifflin Company, 2000.

When penguins slide on their bellies in the snow, it is called tobogganing.

INDEX